MW01087734

ISBN: 9781097626120

a tale of healing and self-love

you are enough.
you are enough.
you are enough.
you are enough.
you are enough.
you are enough.

written by:
vp wright

to all the young girls
who were always told
they were never
good enough.

"be the role model that you
needed when you were young."

growing up i allowed people to tell me words that not only *broke* my spirit but internally darkened my soul.

i **hated** myself.

i used to come home crying to my parents. i would ask why i wasn't liked by people. why i was different. why i couldn't "be like everyone else."

by the time i was twelve years old, i was suffering from depression, anxiety, and had suicidal thoughts and tendencies that followed me into my collegiate years.

i was absolutely ***broken***.

i was in need of serious encouragement and mentorship that i personally did not receive until i went off to college and began finding myself through my education and personal development.

what i was blessed with -- and what ended up saving my life -- isn't always available to girls and young women like me. in fact, it was almost impossible to find the words i needed to hear prior to leaving my adolescent years.

i wish i had these reminders with me when i felt like *i wasn't enough*. when i felt like i wasn't *pretty* enough, *worthy* enough, or *good* enough for positive things to occur in my life. when i felt like i didn't deserve to be happy. i always felt like i had to work ten times harder to get two steps forward, only to be thrown back again.

you deserve *grace and mercy*. you deserve *forgiveness*, so please start learning how to forgive yourself. please remember that there are things in life we cannot control, and that the universe is so massive that the little things won't matter tomorrow. please remember to smile more.

please don't let anyone outside of you control your quality of life. there are only so many days you have on this earth. you deserve to spend them happy.

i hope this book reaches you at the precise moment that you needed it.

i hope you keep a copy in your purse, backpack, on your phone, or on your tablet. i hope you pull it out when you need to be reminded that you are more than enough.

i hope my words are what you need to see. i know for me, what i know now would have saved me so much time, tears, and heartbreak as a child.

but if i hadn't experienced the hurt then, i never would have healed and been able to share these words with you now.

you deserve to be here. *you matter*.

        - vp wright

Table of Contents

i couldn't say these
words to
myself,

hopefully
writing them
will help
heal
someone else.

- vp wright

you are enough.

you are enough.

you are *more* than
enough.

please,
don't let
anyone else
tell you
other wise.

you are unique.

you are unique.

you were made
to be your own
being.

no duplication
could come close
to your
preciseness.

you are perfect.

you are perfect.

and no,
i don't mean
the kind of
photoshop perfection
you see on
magazines
and
tv screens.

i mean perfectly
in your space,
every hair on your head
placed,
your
crooked smile
brightens days
and you don't need
likes and comments
to take someone's
breath away.

you are intelligent.

you are intelligent.

and your intelligence
only adds to your
ability to shine.

your quest for knowledge
is admirable
and craved by others.

you're teased for
raising your hand
too often,

yet no one ever
compliments you
for wanting more
than to know enough.

you are wanted.

you are wanted.

it may not seem like it,
but you are.

i know right now
feels lonely
and you can't seem to
find someone who
gets you.

you can't seem to
find someone
who is into you
as much
as you are
them.

and it may be hard,
but one day
they will come.

and you won't feel
lonely anymore.

the best thing you can do
right now

is work on
becoming whole
for yourself

instead of *waiting* and
wanting
for someone to
make you feel
whole.

you are worthy.

you are worthy.

you are worthy of life.

no matter the color of
your melanin,
the way your
body moves
or how it doesn't.

no matter
the thoughts
in your head
created by others.

no matter what society
says
about who you are,
where you come from,
or what you do.

no matter
who may
like you
or
not like you.

no matter if you
look like.
talk like,
act like,
other girls of
your race
or don't.

no matter your
ambiguous features.

no matter your
sexuality or
gender expression.

no matter
if the so called
"Christians"
on the corner
say God hates you.

no matter
if you are
poor and broken.

no matter the sin
that covers
your spirit.

no matter what
matters,
all that matters
is the
love
you are
worthy of.

you are compassionate.

you are compassionate.

you were there when
no one else was.

when new students
were scared of their
environment.

when bullies wouldn't
leave your friends alone.

when teachers didn't
believe in
you
or
your classmates.

when someone
needed you
to be
their voice.

you were there when
it was just you alone.

facing a large world for
the sake of others
who were afraid of
deportation
or
misrepresentation.

before
activist culture
was in
and
protesting
was fashionable.

you were there to make
a difference.

don't let the world
snuff you out.

you are a healer.

you are a healer.

you have the ability to
bring peace
over those ridden with
anxiety, depression
and illness.

you contain
ancestral knowledge
passed down
from your mother
and her mother.

they tried to rid you
of your culture,
your history,

yet they need you
to guide them
through
sickness and
health.

you are powerful.

you are powerful.

you have the power
to give birth
to life.

the power to
influence
peace and war.

the power to
be more than
a mother,

but a leader,
a teacher,
a lover,
a fighter.

you are what
changes cultures
and are often
not given the
credit.

you can be
president or vice-president
but the choice
on which one it will be,
will be
yours
and not
theirs.

you have the power
to run a company
while raising
your family.

you have the power to
guide your household
in love and faith.

you have the power
to seduce and conquer.

you have the power
to be unstoppable.

you have more power
than you thought
you did,

and the only reason
you haven't
wreaked havoc
on those
who told you
you didn't have
said power,

is because you
believed them.

you are beautiful.

you are beautiful.

in case no one told you,
please do not forget.

don't let anyone
tell you that
you are not.

don't let social media
dim your light
or
gray your sway.

don't nitpick away
at what you call
your "flaws."

you are made in an
image far greater than
anything in this
universe.

you are able.

you are able.

you can do anything
you put your
mind to.

through
time and *determination*,
through
consistency and *hard work*,
through
prayer and *patience*,

you are able
to do
whatever you want
to do
just continue to

push through.

you are loved.

you are loved.

you are loved by
a creator
we will never see
while living
but will inevitably see
in death.

you are loved by
friends and
admirers.

you are loved by a planet
that gives you air to
breath,
water to
drink,
land to
inhabit,
and materials to
create with.

you are loved by
the sun.
it shines down on you
and makes your melanin
pop all year long.

you are loved by
vultures
who steal your culture
while watching you
from afar.

you are loved
unconditionally
in so many ways,

yet you placed conditions
on yourself
because
someone taught them
to you.

you are warm.

you are warm.

you make your lovers
melt into your
essence.

you have a fire in
your heart
that burns
brightly.

people turn their
heads
when they feel your
presence.

yet you believe
you're only noticed
slightly.

you bring joy.

you bring joy.

your laugh is infectious.
your jokes --
no matter how awful --
always bring a smile to
someone's face.

you're no class clown,
but your humor
is appreciated.

you make someone's day,
everyday.

you are loyal.

you are loyal.

you can be
counted on.

you are appreciated
even if no one has
told you so.

someone can call you
and you'll pick up the phone.

someone can depend on you
to be a
shoulder
to lean on.

i know it feels like
you don't
have that for yourself.

i know how isolating it feels,
to be used
but not heard.

you are honest.

you are honest.

you tell the truth.
even when you know
it may hurt
someone you care about.

even though it may break
someone's heart.

even though it may
make someone
uncomfortable.

you are blunt.
you don't hold back.
you are not a bitch.

you just value *truth*
over *bullshit*.

you are pure.

you are pure.

you were violated
and abused,
but you are not
a victim.

you are a *victor*.
you are a *survivor*.
you are *pure*.

you are worthy of
love and affection.

your body is
a temple.
untainted,
and built on
a fruitful foundation.

you are more than
what they did to you.

you are a protector.

you are a protector.

i know it feels like
you have to work
harder
than your peers
over and over again.

you have to prove yourself
repeatedly,
in order to be believed
that you are
capable.

you have to out yourself
in order to evaluate if
you are truly in
a safe situation.

you have to constantly
wear your
identity
on your sleeve
in order to
protect yourself.

you've mastered the skills of
codeswitching
and
picking your battles
when you find yourself
in places
not friendly to you.

you know how to
defend yourself
if attacked
physically,
mentally,
or emotionally,
because you had to learn.

your cautious of
people
when earning your
trust,
because you've been hurt
before.

you are stronger
than you give
yourself
credit for
and it's all because
you learned
lessons
you thought would
break you.

you became your own
bodyguard
when the one you
trusted
failed you.

you are *brave*.

you are talented.

you are talented.

don't let rejection
deter you from developing
your gift(s).

you put in time and effort
in perfecting your craft.

not everyone will appreciate
how much pressure
you had to put on
yourself
to make a
diamond.

you are human.

you are human.

perfect by design,
yet, imperfect by
your decisions
and actions.

you make mistakes,
and that's okay.

you will fail,
but you are not
a failure.

you will fall,
but you will not
stay on the ground
forever.

rock bottom isn't
so bad
when the way back
to being okay
feels so good.

you will hurt,
but you will heal.

there will be battles
you will lose,
but the war
is not over.

you will live.
you will win.
you will succeed.

life is not easy
and it never
will be.

but it is
worth it.

it is always
worth it.

you can find more poetry by vp wright
at www.vpwright.com
@thevpwright
#diaryofablackmillennial

Made in the USA
Middletown, DE
14 January 2023

22172633R00038